BEST.
ROAD TRIP.
JOKES.
EVER.

JOKES for KIDS

CHANTELLE GRACE

BroadStreet
KIDS

BroadStreet Kids
Savage, Minnesota, USA

BroadStreet Kids is an imprint of
BroadStreet Publishing Group, LLC.
Broadstreetpublishing.com

Best Road Trip Jokes Ever

© 2020 by BroadStreet Publishing®

978-1-4245-6087-5
978-1-4245-6088-2 (ebook)

Content compiled by Chantelle Grace.

Design by Chris Garborg | garborgdesign.com

Editorial services by Michelle Winger | literallyprecise.com

Printed in the United States of America.

20   21   22   23   24   25   7   6   5   4   3   2   1

Author Bio

CHANTELLE GRACE is a witty wordsmith who loves music, art, and competitive games. She is also fascinated by God's intricate design of the human body. As a recent graduate from The University of Auckland with a degree in Nursing, she knows it's important to share the gift of laughter with those around her. Although she grew up in the frozen tundra of Minnesota, she currently resides in the beautiful country of New Zealand where she works as a registered nurse.

ON THE ROAD AGAIN

What goes through towns, up hills, and down hills but never moves?

The road.

What is the highest road?

The highway.

What do you get when two giraffes collide?

A giraffic jam.

Why did the zebra cross the road?

Because it was a zebra crossing.

Why did the rhino get a ticket?

He ran through the stomp sign.

What did the stoplight say to the car?

"Don't look, I'm about to change."

Why did the elephant cross the road?

Because the chicken retired.

Why did Superman cross the road?

To get to the supermarket.

Why did the rhino cross the road?

To prove to the possum that it could be done.

How does a snowman get around?

He rides an icicle.

Why did the horse cross the road?

Because somebody shouted hay.

How do billboards talk?

Sign language.

The taxi driver was good at his job.

He kept driving his customers away.

AT SEA

What does a houseboat turn into when it grows up?

A township.

What's the worst vegetable to serve on a boat?

Leeks.

What floats in water and wears a uniform?

A buoy scout.

What do you call discounts at the boat store?

A two for one sail.

What do you call it when one hundred people stand on a dock?

Pier pressure.

What happened to the sailor when he did poorly on a test?

He got C-sick.

What did the sailor say when he was accused of speeding on his boat?

"I did knot."

What did the sailor use to buy his boat?

Sand dollars.

What is another name for a captain of a sailboat.

A sails manager.

Where do sick boats go?

The dock.

If a boat could fly, where would it go?

An airport.

What is in the middle of the ocean?

The letter E.

Where did Bugs Bunny anchor his boat?

At the what's-up dock.

What kind of candy would help
someone who fell off a boat?

A lifesaver.

What runs but never walks?

Water.

Why don't oysters share their pearls?

Because they're shellfish.

Why did the lobster go red?

It saw the ocean's bottom.

What kind of rocks are never found in the ocean?

Dry ones.

Why is the ocean measured in knots instead of miles?

They need to keep the ocean tide.

Why did the teacher dive into the ocean?

To test the water.

What do you use to cut the ocean in half?

A sea-saw.

Why does the octopus always laugh?

He has ten-tickles.

What turtle is the easiest to see?

A sea turtle.

What is the most famous fish in the ocean?

The starfish.

Where does a killer whale go to the dentist?

The Orcadontist.

What puts white lines on the ocean?

An ocean liner.

What kind of hair do oceans have?

Wavy.

Have you heard of seasickness?

It comes in waves.

What lies at the bottom of the ocean
and twitches?

A nervous wreck.

What do you get when you throw one
million books into the ocean?

Title waves.

What do you get if you cross an elephant with a whale?

A submarine with a built-in snorkel.

How much money does a pirate pay for corn?

A buccaneer.

BY AIR

Heard about the pilot who decided to cook while flying?

It was a recipe for disaster.

Why couldn't the librarian get on the plane?

Because it was overbooked.

What kind of chocolate do they sell at the airport?

Plane chocolate.

What happens when you wear a watch on a plane?

Time flies.

Why did the airplane get sent to its room?

It had a bad altitude.

Where do mountain climbers keep their planes?

Cliffhangers.

What has a nose and can fly, but cannot smell?

A plane.

Why did the student study on a plane?

To get higher grades.

What do you get when you cross a dog and an airplane?

A jet setter.

What's gray and moves at one hundred miles an hour?

A jet-propelled elephant.

What do you call an elephant that flies?

A jumbo jet.

What happened to the guy who sued over his missing luggage?

He lost his case.

A photon was traveling through airport security. The TSA agent asked if he had any luggage. The photon said...

"No, I'm traveling light."

IN TRAINING

How does a train eat?

It chew chews.

When is a rabbit as fast as a train?

When it's on the train.

What did the train conductor get for her birthday?

Platform shoes.

How do trains hear?

With engineers.

How do you find a missing train?

Follow the tracks.

What do you call a train that sneezes?

Achoo-choo train.

Why was the train late?

It kept getting side-tracked.

What is as big as a train, but weighs nothing?

Its shadow.

Why don't elephants like trains?

They can't leave their trunks in the baggage car.

Why was the train humming?

It didn't remember the words to the song.

HORSE AND CART

Why did the pony have to gargle?

Because it was a little horse.

What did the horse say when it fell?

"I've fallen and I can't giddyup."

When does a horse talk?

Whinney wants to.

What do you call a horse that lives next door?

A neigh-bor.

What's the best way to lead a horse to water?

With lots of apples and carrots.

What disease was the horse afraid of getting?

Hay fever.

How long should a horse's legs be?

Long enough to reach the ground.

Why did the man stand behind the horse?

He was hoping to get a kick out of it.

Which horse is the most mysterious?

Black Beauty. He's a dark horse.

What does it mean if you find a horseshoe?

Some poor horse is walking around in his socks.

What do you call a well-balanced horse?

Stable.

What do you give a sick horse?

Cough stirrup.

What is the difference between a horse and a duck?

One goes quick and the other goes quack.

What's a horse's favorite sport?

Stable tennis.

Why do cowboys ride horses?

Because they're too heavy to carry.

Where do horses go when they're sick?

The horsepital.

Why did the horse eat with its mouth open?

Because it had bad stable manners.

What do you call a scary female horse?

A nightmare.

What do you call a horse that can't lose a race?

Sherbet.

What street do horses live on?

Mane St.

What did the momma say to the foal?

"It's pasture bedtime."

What did the mare tell her filly after dinner?

Clear the stable.

What kind of bread does a horse eat?

Thoroughbred.

What is the difference between a horse and the weather?

One is reined up and the other rains down.

CROSS COUNTRY

Which state is the happiest?

Merry-land.

What did Dela-ware?

A New Jersey.

Which state is the loudest?

Illi-noise.

What state is round on the outsides and high on the inside?

Ohio.

What did Tennessee?

The same as Arkansas.

Where do math teachers go on vacation?

Times Square.

Where do crayons go on vacation?

Color-ado.

Where do you go to dance in California?

San Frandisco.

What state produces cheese?

Swiss-consin.

What is a horse's favorite state?

Neighbraska.

Which state does the most laundry?

Washington.

What has four eyes but can't see?

Mississippi.

Where do eggs go on vacation?

New Yolk City.

Which state is the smartest?

Alabama because it has four As and one B.

What would you call the US if everyone lived in their cars?

An in-car-nation.

Why is it so easy to get into Florida?

Because of all the keys.

What state makes the country's pencils?

Pennsylvania.

Where do horses get their hair done?

Maine.

Which state is famous for its small soft drinks?

Mini-soda.

Where do cows go on their summer vacation?

Moo York.

What is a lion's favorite state?

Maine.

Why did the cow go to California?

To see where moovies are filmed.

Where do pianists go for vacation?

Florida Keys

What rock group has four men who
don't sing?

Mt. Rushmore.

AROUND THE WORLD

What travels around the world but stays in one corner?

A stamp.

What did the Pacific Ocean say to the Atlantic Ocean?

Nothing. It just waved.

Where is the biggest rope in the world?

Europe.

Where can you find the biggest pans in the world?

Japan.

Where do pirates go for vacation?

Arrrgentina.

Which country is the fastest?

Russia.

What country leaves the biggest mark?

Denmark.

What's the coldest country in the world?

Chile.

What country does Hungary eat?

Turkey.

Are you going to visit Egypt?

I sphinx so.

Do you want to eat your food here?

No, I want it Togo.

What do you call the little rivers that flow into the Nile?

Juveniles.

Is traveling to Costa Rica expensive?

It costa fortune.

Why is England the wettest country?

Because royalty has reigned there for years.

Where does pizza go on vacation?

The Leaning Tower of Pizza.

Where do sheep go for vacation?

The Baahamas.

Where do sharks go on vacation?

Finland.

Where do hamsters go on vacation?

Hamsterdam.

Where do bees go on vacation?

Stingapore.

Where does a bird like to travel?

The Canary Islands.

What is an ant's favorite vacation spot?

Frants.

What do you call a French man in sandals?

Phillipe Phloppe.

What do you take on a trip to the desert?

A thirst-aid kit.

What did the envelope say to the stamp?

"Stick with me and we'll go places."

What do you call a Spanish man who lost his car?

Carlos.

What do you call an elephant at the North Pole?

Cold.

Did you know French fries weren't actually cooked in France?

They were cooked in Greece.

Which country's capital has the fastest growing population?

Ireland. Every day it's Dublin.

What city cheats on tests?

Peking.

Visitors to Cuba are usually...

Havana good time.

I have a lengthy article on Japanese Sword Fighters...

I can Samurais it for you.

England doesn't have a kidney bank.

It has a Liverpool.

He said he was from South America.

I said, "I don't Bolivia."

Italian building inspectors in Pisa...

are lenient.

In a Scandinavian race, the last Lapp...

crossed the Finnish line.

Goats in France are musical.

They have French horns.

Things made in Australia...

are high koala-ty.

If you Russia round and Ukraine your neck...

don't Crimea River.

I would like to go to Holland one day.

Wooden shoe?

When I go to West Africa...

I'm Ghana make sure Togo to Mali and then I can say I've Benin Timbuktu.

There is some Confucion about...

the oldest religion in China.

Television sets in Great Britain...

have to cross the English Channel.

You don't know anything at all about ancient Egypt?

Tut, tut, tut.

The pharaohs of Egypt...

worked on the first pyramid scheme.

Which country has the most germs?

Germany.

Where were donuts first made?

In Greece.

Why did the Romanian stop reading?

To give her Bucharest.

If you send a letter to the Philippines...

you should put it in a Manila envelope.

People are happy when they vacation in Ireland.

They're usually walking on Eire.

People in Switzerland learn to ski...

with a lot of alp.

The US government has a lot of red tape.

In Scotland, they use Scotch tape.

. . . .

MAP IT OUT

Why are maps like fish?

They both have scales.

What kind of map plays CDs?

A stereo map.

Why was the map gesturing wildly?

It was an animated map.

What do you get when you cross a farm animal with a map maker?

A cowtographer.

What does a great sportsman and map key have in common?

They're legends.

What do you call a man on top of a hill?

Cliff.

Did you hear the mountain joke?

No one can get over it.

Why are rivers rich?

They have two banks.

What do you find in the middle of nowhere?

The letter H.

What is a mountain's favorite type of candy?

Snow caps.

What did one volcano say to the other?

"I lava you."

Why are mountains the funniest place to travel?

They're hill areas.

TO THE MECHANIC

What has three letters and starts with gas?

A car.

What is a car's favorite meal?

Brake-fast.

Why should you check your car's tires for holes?

Because there might be a fork in the road.

What part of the car is the laziest?

The wheels because they're always tired.

When is a car not a car?

When it turns into the driveway.

What do you call a man with a car on his head?

Jack.

Why couldn't the car play soccer?

It only had one boot.

What was wrong with the wooden car?

It wooden go.

Why did the mechanic sleep
under the car?

He wanted to wake up oily.

What has four wheels and flies?

A garbage truck.

Where do old Volkswagen cars go?

The old Volks home.

What happened when the frog's car
broke down?

He started to jump it.

What made the dinosaur's car stop?

A flat Tireannosaurus.

What happens to a frog's car when it breaks down?

It gets toad.

My sister told me I couldn't make a car out of spaghetti.

You should have seen her face as I drove pasta.

I'm trying to make a car without wheels.

I've been working on it tirelessly.

I couldn't figure out how to buckle my seat belt.

Then it clicked.

WEATHER FORECAST

How does a hurricane see?

With its eye.

What happens before a candy storm?

It sprinkles.

When does it rain money?

When there is change in the weather.

What did one lightning bolt say to the other?

"You're shocking."

What type of cloud is lazy because it never gets up?

Fog.

What does the cloud wear under its pants?

Thunder-wear.

What's worse than raining cats and dogs?

Hailing taxis.

What bow can't be tied?

A rainbow.

What do clouds do when they're rich?

They make it rain.

What did the tornado say to the sports car?

"Want to go for a spin?"

Can bees fly in the rain?

Not without their yellow jackets.

What do you call it when it rains chickens and ducks?

Foul weather.

What did one blade of grass say to the other about the lack of rain?

I guess we'll just have to make dew.

I tried to catch the fog the other day.

I mist.

TROPICAL VACATION

Two waves had a race, who won?

They tide.

What did the beach say when the tide came in?

"Long time no sea."

What is brown, hairy, and wears sunglasses?

A coconut on vacation.

What kind of tree can you hold in your hand?

A palm tree.

What do you pay to spend a day on the beach?

Sand dollars.

What is the best kind of sandwich for the beach?

A peanut butter and jellyfish.

What's the best day to go to the beach?

Sun-day.

What did one tide pool say to the other?

"Show me your mussels."

Why do bananas use sunscreen at the beach?

Because they peel.

Why couldn't the two elephants go swimming together?

Because they only had one pair of trunks.

What does bread do on vacation?

It loaves around.

What's black and white and red all over?

A sun-burned zebra.

What does Cinderella wear when she goes to the beach?

Glass flippers.

What does the sun drink out of?

Sunglasses.

Why can't basketball players go to the beach?

They'd get called for travelling.

Why did the robot go on a beach vacation?

He needed to recharge his batteries.

What does Baloo the Bear pack for a trip to the beach?

Just the bear necessities.

What do frogs like to drink on a hot summer's day?

Croak-a-Cola!

How do rabbits get to their beach vacation?

By hare-plane!

What kind of shoes does a person wear on a vacation?

Loafers

CAMPOUT

How do you start a fire using two pieces of wood?

Make sure one is a matchstick.

Can a frog jump higher than a tent?

Of course. Tents can't jump.

What did one campfire say to the other?

"Do you want to go out tonight?"

Did you hear about the fire at the campsite?

It was intents.

What's another name for a sleeping bag?

A nap sack.

Why does Humpty Dumpty love camping in autumn?

Because he had a great fall.

Why are people who go camping on April 1st always tired?

Because they just finished a 31-day March.

What is a tree's favorite drink?

Root beer.

What did the doctor tell the camper when he went to the hospital?

You're two tents.

What did the alpaca say to his owner before camping?

"Alpaca tent."

What color is the wind?

Blew.

How do you catch a squirrel?

Climb a tree and act like a nut.

If you have five tents in one hand and three in the other, what do you have?

Very big hands.

What do you call a camper without a nose and a body?

Nobody nose.

Why do trees have so many friends?

Because they branch out.

Why are hiking shops so diverse?

Because they hire people from all walks of life.

I didn't like the romantic tree movie.

It was far too sappy.

How do you keep your sleeping bag
from getting stretched out?

Don't sleep too long in it.

If you're in the woods, how can you tell
if a tree is a dogwood?

By its bark.

What do bears call campers
in sleeping bags?

Soft tacos.

If you're on a hike and find a fork in the
road, what do you do?

Stop for lunch.

You can't run through a campsite.

You can only "ran" because it's past tents.

I went to buy camping camouflage yesterday.

I couldn't find any.

The seaside camping trip was so boring.

One day the tide went out and never came back.

If you get cold while camping, sit in the corner of a tent.

It's usually 90 degrees.

FISHING TRIP

What does a lion do on a canoe?

Use his roar.

Why did the melon jump into the lake?

Because he wanted to be a watermelon.

Why did the fish blush?

Because it saw the lake's bottom.

What did the beaver say to the tree?

"It's been nice gnawing you."

How do you avoid getting swallowed by a river while kayaking?

Stay away from its mouth.

What is a fisherman's favorite show?

The Reel Life.

How do you catch a fish without a fishing rod?

With bear hands.

Do fish go on vacation?

No, because they're always in school.

What do you call waiting five hours to catch a fish on a boat?

Quick.

What is the best way to communicate with a fish?

Drop it a line.

Why do oars fall in love?

Because they're rowmantic.

WILDLIFE SIGHTINGS

What sports car do cats drive?

Furaris.

What's a frog's favorite car?

A beetle.

What is a sheep's favorite car?

A Lamborghini.

What kind of cars do snakes drive?

Anahondas.

What kind of cars do dogs hate?

Corvets.

What do you call it when dinosaurs crash their cars?

Tyrannosaurus wrecks.

Why are pigs bad drivers?

They hog the road.

Where do dogs park their cars?

The barking lot.

What is a cow's favorite holiday?

Moo Year's Eve.

Why did the spider cross the road?

To get to her website.

What do you call a flying primate?

A hot air baboon.

Why did the whales cross the ocean?

To get to the other tide.

What is gray, has four legs and a trunk?

A mouse on vacation.

What do you say to a frog who needs a ride?

"Hop in."

How do fleas travel from place to place?

Itch-hiking.

What snakes are found on cars?

Windshield vipers.

Where did the goldfish go on vacation?

Around the globe.

Why do birds fly south in the winter?

Because it's too far to walk.

What would you call gulls that fly over the bay, instead of the sea?

Bagels.

Why do elephants have trunks?

Because they would look funny with a suitcase.

What did the elephant say to her son when he was naughty in the car?

"Tusk tusk."

What do you call a bee that can't make up its mind?

A maybe.

What do you call a thieving alligator?

A crookodile.

What do you call a pig that does karate?

Pork chop.

PACK A BOOK

Traveling

by Anna Plane

Parachuting

by Hugo First

I Need Insurance

by Justin Case

Flying for Beginners

by Landon Safely

Where to Stay while Traveling

by Moe Tell

Mosquito Bites

by Ivan Itch

Vacation Budgeting

by Seymour Forles

How to Sail

by Boe Ting

A Perfect Day for Sailing

by Wynn Dee

Runaway Horse

by A. Tailov Woh

Daddy Are We There Yet?

by Miles Away

Stop Arguing

by Xavier Breath

Downpour

by Wayne Dwops

Life in Chicago

by Wendy City

Sea Birds

by Al Batross

Danger

by Luke Out

I'm Fine

by Howard Yu

Get Moving

by Sheik Aleg

I Like Fish

by Ann Chovie

I Must Fix the Car

by Otto Doit

Why Cars Stop

by M.T. Tank

It's Unfair

by Y. Me

Falling Trees

by Tim Burr

I Love Crowds

by Morris Merrier

Highway Travel

by Dusty Rhodes

Without Warning

by Oliver Sudden

Desert Crossing

by I. Rhoda Camel

You're Kidding

by Shirley U. Jest

I Say So

by Frank O. Pinion

Mountain Climbing

by Andover Hand

Equine Leg Cramps

by Charlie Horse

Exercise on Wheels

by Cy Kling

In the Arctic Ocean

by Isa Berg

Turtle Racing

by Eubie Quick

Almost Missed the Bus

by Justin Time

Where to Find Islands

by Archie Pelago

French Overpopulation

by Francis Crowded

The Excitement of Trees

by I. M. Board

Bundle of Laughs

by Vera Funny

WE'VE ARRIVED

Knock, knock?

Who's there?

Alaska.

Alaska who?

Alaska later, right now I'm busy.

Knock, knock.

Who's there?

Norway.

Norway who?

*Norway am I telling you any more
knock, knock jokes.*

Knock, knock.

Who's there?

Oman.

Oman who?

Oman, these jokes are bad.

Knock, knock.

Who's there?

Kenya.

Kenya who?

Kenya think of a better joke?

Knock, knock.

Who's there?

Francis.

Francis who?

Francis a country in Europe.

Knock, knock.

Who's there?

Canoe.

Canoe who?

Canoe come over and play?

Knock, knock.

Who's there?

Lettuce.

Lettuce who?

Lettuce in; it's cold outside.

Knock, knock.

Who's there?

Avenue.

Avenue who?

Avenue heard this joke before?

Knock, knock.

Who's there?

Water.

Water who?

Water way to answer the door.

Knock, knock.

Who's there?

Havana.

Havana who?

Havana good time and wishing you were here.

Knock, knock.

Who's there?

Ida.

Ida who?

It's pronounced Idaho.

Knock, knock.

Who's there?

Juneau.

Juneau who?

Juneau the capital of Alaska?

Knock, knock.

Who's there?

Oslo.

Oslo who?

Oslo down. No need to hurry.

Knock, knock.

Who's there?

Venice.

Venice who?

Venice mom coming home?

Knock, knock.

Who's there?

Cargo.

Cargo who?

Cargo better if you fill it with gas first.

Knock, knock.

Who's there?

Iona.

Iona who?

Iona new car.

Knock, knock.

Who's there?

Isabel.

Isabel who?

Isabel necessary for riding a bike?

Knock, knock.

Who's there?

Ivan.

Ivan who?

Ivan working all day.

Knock, knock.

Who's there?

Levin.

Levin who?

Levin on a jet plane.

Knock, knock.

Who's there?

Philip.

Philip who?

Philip my gas tank, please. I've got a long way to go.

LICENSE PLATES

On a Tesla:

OIL LOL

On an Infiniti:

N BYOND

On a Ferrari:

ESCUZME

On a smart car:

OH I FIT

On a Saab:

WHASAAB

On a Delorean:

TIMELESS

On a VW Beetle:

EW A BUG

On a yellow car:

PIKACHU

On a Cube:

RUBIX

• • • • • • • • • • • •

WRITE YOUR
FAVORITE JOKE HERE